The Foundations of Blooming

Master the Secrets of Fertile Soil to Maximize Your Vegetable Garden's Productivity

©Jean-Pierre Lavigne, 2023
All rights reserved. No part of this book may be reproduced or transmitted in any form or by any means, electronic or mechanical, including photocopying, recording or any information storage system, without the written permission of the author, except for a brief quotation in a review or newspaper article.

Contents

Introduction 5
The Importance of Fertile Soil for a Productive Garden 5
Objectives of the Book 6

Understanding the Basics of Soil 9
Soil Structure and its Role in Fertility 9
Different Types of Soils and Their Properties 10
Components of Soil: Minerals, Organic Matter, Air, and Water 12

Life in the Soil 14
Soil Organisms: Bacteria, Fungi, Protozoa, Nematodes, and Microarthropods ... 14
The Importance of Soil Microorganisms 15
Decomposers and their Role in Humus Formation 17
Symbioses and Interactions between Plants and Soil Organisms 18

Essential Nutrients for Plants and Soil Chemistry 20
The essential macronutrients: nitrogen, phosphorus, and potassium 20
Micronutrients and their role in plant growth 21
The importance of nutrient balance 23
Soil pH and its influence on nutrient availability 24

Soil Analysis and Interpretation 26
Soil Sampling Methods 26
Soil Testing and its Results 27
Understanding Soil Analysis Results 28

Natural Amendments and Fertilizers 30
Soil Amendment to Correct pH and Nutrient Deficiencies 30
Different Categories of Amendments 31
How to Adapt Amendments Based on Soil Analysis Results 33

The Importance of Organic Matter in the Soil 34
Organic Fertilizers: Manure, Compost, Guano, etc. 35
Mineral Fertilizers: Limestone, Magnesium Sulfate, etc. 37

Improving Soil Fertility Naturally 39

The Composting Process and Best Composting Practices 39
Cover Crops and Green Manure 40
The Benefits of Cover Crops 42
The Use of Mycorrhizae and Nitrogen-Fixing Bacteria 43

Soil Fertility Improvement Techniques 45

Crop Rotation and Companion Planting 45
Soil Management: Tillage, Aeration, Mulching 46
Agroforestry and Intercropping 48

The Role of Plants in Soil Fertility 50

Nitrogen-Fixing Plants 50
Soil-Loosening and Soil-Improving Plants 51
Soil Quality Indicator Plants 52

Advanced Techniques to Maximize Garden Productivity 54

Permaculture and Its Basic Principles 54
Aquaponics and Hydroponic Cultivation 56
Biodynamics and the Use of Biodynamic Preparations 57

Water and Irrigation Management 59

The Importance of Water in the Soil 59
Understanding Plant Water Needs 60
Different Irrigation Techniques and Their Impact on Soil Fertility 61
Water Conservation and Resource Management 62
Drainage and Excess Water Management 63

Prevention and Control of Pests, Diseases, and Soil Problems .. 66

The Enemies of the Soil 66
Techniques for Managing Soil Diseases and Pests 67
The Importance of Biodiversity and Garden Allies 68
Identifying and Correcting Nutrient Deficiencies 69

Common Soil Problems and How to Solve Them 72

Acidic and Alkaline Soils: Causes and Consequences 72
Managing Salinity and Acidic or Alkaline Soils 73
Compacted Soils: Causes, Consequences, and Solutions 74
Polluted Soils: Causes, Consequences, and Solutions 75

Growing Plants Adapted to Your Soil and Climate 77

Choosing Resilient and Locally Adapted Varieties 77
The Importance of Pollination and Selecting Bee-Friendly Plants 78
Permaculture and the Design of Productive and Sustainable Gardens 79

Case Studies and Testimonials from Expert Gardeners 82

Successful experiences of gardens that have improved soil fertility 82
Research projects and innovations in soil fertility 83
Experiences of farmers and professional gardeners 85
Tips and tricks from experienced gardeners 86
Acknowledgment 89

Introduction

The Importance of Fertile Soil for a Productive Garden

Soil is the foundation of all agricultural and gardening production. Fertile soil provides plants with the necessary nutrients for healthy and vigorous growth, optimal drainage conditions, and a habitat for beneficial soil organisms. On the other hand, poor soil can lead to plant diseases, low yields, and high costs in fertilizers and pesticides.

Having fertile soil is therefore crucial for maximizing the productivity of a garden. Plants need a favorable soil environment to absorb the nutrients, water, and oxygen they need to grow, develop, and produce high-quality fruits and vegetables.

Fertile soil is also important for the overall health of the environment. Fertile soils contain a large amount of organic matter, which contributes to water retention, regulates soil temperature, and reduces erosion. Plants grown on fertile soils are also more resistant to diseases and pests, reducing the need for pesticides.

Furthermore, fertile soils have a positive impact on the quality of food produced. Nutrients present in the soil are absorbed by plants and transferred to fruits and vegetables. Thus, nutrient-rich soil can have a direct effect on the flavor and quality of food products.

It is therefore essential for every gardener, amateur or professional, to understand the components of fertile soil and how to maintain them in optimal condition. This not only maximizes yields but also contributes to environmental preservation and the production of healthy and nutritious food.

Objectives of the Book

The objectives of this book are multiple and aim to help amateur gardeners maximize the productivity of their gardens by understanding and mastering the secrets of fertile soil. Firstly, we want to raise awareness among readers about the importance of fertile soil for a productive garden. We also aim to help gardeners understand the basics of soil by exploring its structure, different types, and properties, as well as its essential components such as minerals, organic matter, air, and water.

We also wish to provide clear and detailed information about soil life and the different organisms residing in it, as well as the importance of these organisms for soil fertility. We will also examine essential plant nutrients and soil chemistry, emphasizing the importance of balancing nutrients and soil pH.

An important part of this book will be dedicated to soil analysis and interpretation, as well as the use of amendments and natural fertilizers to correct nutrient deficiencies and adjust soil pH. We will also discuss techniques for naturally improving soil fertility, such as composting, cover cropping, green manures, mycorrhizae, and nitrogen-fixing bacteria.

We will explore cultivation techniques to enhance soil fertility, addressing topics such as crop rotation, companion planting, soil tillage, agroforestry, and intercropping.

An important part of this book will also be devoted to plants and their role in soil fertility, examining nitrogen-fixing plants, soil-remediating and improving plants, as well as plants that indicate soil quality.

We also wish to present advanced techniques for maximizing garden productivity, such as permaculture, aquaponics, hydroponics, biodynamics, and the use of biodynamic preparations.

We will also cover topics such as water management and irrigation, prevention and control of pests, diseases, and soil problems, as well as common soil issues and how to solve them.

Finally, we aim to inspire readers with case studies and testimonials from expert gardeners, sharing their successful experiences and tips and tricks.

Overall, this book aims to provide amateur gardeners with a comprehensive understanding of soil fertility and techniques to maximize their garden's productivity. We hope that the information presented in this book will be helpful, practical, and inspiring for all passionate gardeners seeking to improve their practice.

Understanding the Basics of Soil

Soil Structure and its Role in Fertility

Soil structure is a key element of a garden's fertility. It is composed of different layers that interact to provide plants with the nutrients, water, and oxygen they need to grow.

The top layer of soil is called the arable layer. It contains organic matter and microorganisms that break down this organic matter to form humus, a substance that retains water and nutrients in the soil. The arable layer is also responsible for the circulation of water and oxygen in the soil.

Below the arable layer is the transition layer. This layer contains a significant amount of minerals and nutrients that are slowly released into the soil to nourish plants.

Finally, below the transition layer is the rocky substrate layer. This layer is composed of rocks and minerals that provide a solid structure to the soil.

The structure of the soil directly influences the fertility of the garden. Well-structured soil allows plant roots to freely develop and access the necessary nutrients. Additionally, well-structured soil allows for the free circulation of water and oxygen, which is essential for plant growth.

It is important to understand that soil structure can be affected by external factors such as farming practices, weather, and environmental conditions. For example, excessive use of pesticides and chemical fertilizers can disrupt soil structure by killing the microorganisms that live in it. Similarly, prolonged drought can make the soil more compact, limiting water and oxygen circulation.

To maintain a healthy and fertile soil structure, it is important to implement sustainable gardening practices. This includes using organic amendments such as compost and manure to provide organic matter and nutrients to the soil, as well as adopting crop rotation practices to prevent soil nutrient depletion.

Different Types of Soils and Their Properties

Understanding the different types of soils and their properties is key to maximizing the productivity of your garden. There are several different types of soils, each with its own characteristics and properties.

The first type of soil is sandy soil. Sandy soils are composed of relatively coarse sand particles, giving them a gritty and permeable texture. They tend to warm up quickly in the spring and cool down rapidly in the fall, which can be beneficial for certain crops. However, they tend to be very nutrient-poor, as water and nutrients drain quickly through the sand layers. In general, sandy soils require amendments to retain water and nutrients.

The second type of soil is loamy soil. Loamy soils are composed of medium-sized particles, giving them a soft and easily workable texture. They have good water and nutrient retention capacity, making them ideal for many crops. However, they can be prone to compaction, especially if worked when overly wet.

The third type of soil is clay soil. Clay soils are composed of very fine particles, giving them a sticky and heavy texture. They have excellent water and nutrient retention capacity, making them very fertile. However, they can be challenging to work with due to their dense texture and can become very sticky and difficult to cultivate when overly wet. Additionally, they can be prone to compaction if worked when too dry.

The fourth type of soil is limestone soil. Limestone soils are rich in calcium, giving them an alkaline texture and high pH. They are often very fertile and can be highly productive for certain crops. However, they can be challenging to cultivate for plants that prefer more acidic soils.

The fifth type of soil is acidic soil. Acidic soils have a low pH and are often low in calcium and magnesium. They can be challenging to cultivate for plants that prefer more alkaline soils but can be highly productive for others.

Understanding your soil's properties allows you to adapt your gardening practices accordingly. If you are unsure of your soil type, you can seek assistance from a soil expert or use soil tests to help identify your soil's properties.

Components of Soil: Minerals, Organic Matter, Air, and Water

The components of soil are fundamental elements that contribute to soil fertility and are essential for plant growth. Understanding these components is crucial for maximizing the productivity of your garden and maintaining a healthy and fertile soil.

The first component of soil consists of minerals, which are the solid elements of the soil. The most common minerals are sand, clay, and rocks. They also contain essential nutrients for plant growth, such as nitrogen, phosphorus, and potassium. The quantity and quality of minerals in the soil determine its texture, which influences water retention, permeability, and soil aeration. For example, clay soil is more compact and retains more water than sandy soil. However, sandy soil is more permeable and allows for better root aeration.

The second component of soil is organic matter, which comes from the decomposition of plant and animal materials. It contains essential nutrients for plant growth, such as nitrogen, phosphorus, and potassium, as well as trace elements and micronutrients. Organic matter also benefits soil texture by improving water retention and permeability while providing a habitat for soil microorganisms. These microorganisms are necessary for the decomposition of organic matter and the release of nutrients into the soil, contributing to plant growth.

The third component of soil is air, which is crucial for the survival of soil microorganisms and for the respiration of plant roots. Proper soil aeration allows roots to develop properly and facilitates nutrient absorption. Poor soil aeration can lead to the accumulation of carbon dioxide, methane, and other harmful gases in the soil, which can hinder plant growth and soil health.

The fourth and final component of soil is water, which is also essential for plant growth and the survival of soil microorganisms. It is necessary for the dissolution of nutrients in the soil, their transport to the roots, and their absorption by plants. However, excess water can lead to poor soil aeration, anaerobic decomposition, and nutrient loss.

The quantity and quality of each soil component are interdependent and influence soil fertility. For example, an adequate amount of organic matter can improve soil texture, promote water retention, and increase the presence of beneficial microorganisms. On the other hand, an excess of organic matter can lead to poor soil aeration and the accumulation of harmful gases in the soil.

Life in the Soil

Soil Organisms: Bacteria, Fungi, Protozoa, Nematodes, and Microarthropods

Soil organisms are essential for the fertility of your garden. The soil is a complex and dynamic environment, home to billions of microorganisms that work together to maintain soil balance and health. The main soil organisms include bacteria, fungi, protozoa, nematodes, and microarthropods.

Bacteria are single-celled microorganisms present in all soils. They are essential for the decomposition of organic matter, releasing nutrients for plants. Nitrogen-fixing bacteria can transform atmospheric nitrogen into a plant-usable form. Soil bacteria are also involved in the production of plant growth hormones, stimulating plant development.

Fungi are multicellular organisms that play a crucial role in organic matter decomposition in the soil. They produce enzymes that break down organic matter, making it available to plants. Fungi also form symbiotic associations with plant roots, forming mycorrhizae, which increase root absorption surface and enhance nutrient absorption.

Protozoa are single-celled organisms that feed on bacteria and other soil microorganisms. They are also involved in nutrient release for plants through organic matter decomposition.

Nematodes are microscopic worms that feed on bacteria and fungi. Some types of nematodes are beneficial for plants as they protect them from diseases by attacking soil pathogens.

Microarthropods are small animals that live in the soil and feed on organic matter. They contribute to organic matter decomposition and nutrient release for plants.

Together, these microorganisms form a complex ecosystem in the soil, known as «soil biology». They are all interconnected and depend on each other to survive. When this ecosystem is in balance, it can maintain soil health and fertility, allowing plants to grow healthier and faster.

It is important to maintain this balance by using cultivation practices that promote soil life, such as adding organic matter, crop rotation, and reducing pesticide use. By understanding the roles and interactions of soil organisms, you can improve the health of your soil and maximize your garden's productivity.

The Importance of Soil Microorganisms

Soil microorganisms are microscopic living organisms such as bacteria, fungi, protozoa, nematodes, and microarthropods. These living beings play a crucial role in soil fertility and plant health.

Soil microorganisms interact with plants in several ways. Nitrogen-fixing bacteria, for example, work symbiotically with plant roots to provide nitrogen, an essential nutrient, to plants. Mycorrhizal fungi facilitate nutrient absorption by plant roots and contribute to plant growth. Decomposer organisms, such as bacteria and fungi, break down dead organic matter to form humus, a nutrient-rich substance that nourishes plants.

The presence and diversity of soil microorganisms are also essential for plant health. Soil bacteria and fungi act as biological control agents, protecting plants from diseases and pests. Therefore, a high biodiversity of soil microorganisms is necessary to maintain a healthy ecosystem in the soil.

Modern agricultural practices such as excessive use of pesticides and synthetic fertilizers, monoculture, and intensive plowing have reduced soil microorganism biodiversity and led to soil quality degradation. On the other hand, sustainable agricultural practices such as using natural amendments, cover crops, and crop rotation promote soil microorganism biodiversity and improve soil quality.

It is therefore crucial for gardeners to understand the importance of soil microorganisms and take measures to maintain and enhance soil microorganism biodiversity in their garden. This can be accomplished by using natural amendments such as compost, practicing crop rotation, and encouraging biodiversity in the garden by planting plants that attract beneficial insects.

Decomposers and their Role in Humus Formation

Decomposers are soil organisms that play a crucial role in humus formation. These organisms, including bacteria, fungi, protozoa, nematodes, and microarthropods, break down dead organic matter into simpler elements that are then used by plants as nutrient sources.

Bacteria are the primary decomposers in the soil. They are responsible for the rapid decomposition of organic materials. Fungi, on the other hand, decompose organic matter at a slower pace but can break down more resilient organic materials such as dead roots. Protozoa, nematodes, and microarthropods are larger organisms that feed on bacteria and fungi, contributing to nutrient release in the soil.

The decomposition of organic matter by decomposers is a complex process that releases a wide variety of nutrients. The main nutrients released are nitrogen, phosphorus, potassium, calcium, magnesium, sulfur, and other trace elements. These nutrients are essential for plant growth and health.

The decomposed organic matter by decomposers is called humus. Humus is a dark and crumbly material that improves soil structure, promotes water retention and air circulation in the soil, and increases soil's nutrient-holding capacity. Humus is also capable of buffering soil pH fluctuations, which is important for maintaining an optimal environment for plants.

It is important to promote decomposer activity in the soil to maintain fertile soil. For this purpose, it is important to regularly add organic matter to the soil. Organic matter can be added in the form of compost, dead leaves, manure, or other sources. Cover crops and green manure can also help promote decomposer activity.

Symbioses and Interactions between Plants and Soil Organisms

In a garden, plants and soil constantly interact. Plants absorb nutrients and water from the soil, while soil organisms decompose organic matter and produce nutrients for plants. However, interactions between plants and soil organisms go beyond the mere absorption of nutrients.

Some plants have the ability to stimulate the growth of beneficial microorganisms in the soil, while others can repel harmful organisms. These beneficial interactions between plants and soil organisms are called symbioses.

One of the most well-known symbioses is between legumes and nitrogen-fixing bacteria. Legumes, such as beans, peas, and lentils, have the ability to fix atmospheric nitrogen through bacteria present in their roots. In return, these bacteria benefit from the energy produced by the plants for their own growth.

Other plants have the ability to produce chemicals that attract beneficial soil microorganisms, such as bacteria and mycorrhizal fungi. These microorganisms can help plants absorb nutrients and water from the soil, thereby improving their growth and resistance to diseases.

Conversely, some plants are capable of producing chemicals that repel harmful soil organisms such as nematodes and pathogenic fungi. These plants are often used in biological control against soil diseases and pests.

It is important to note that interactions between plants and soil organisms are often specific to each plant and soil organism. Therefore, it is essential to choose the right plants to favor these symbioses in your garden...

Essential Nutrients for Plants and Soil Chemistry

The essential macronutrients: nitrogen, phosphorus, and potassium

The essential macronutrients nitrogen, phosphorus, and potassium are the most important nutrients for plant growth. These elements are required in large quantities to support the growth and production of fruits and vegetables in a garden. Understanding how these macronutrients work and how plants utilize them can help gardeners maximize their garden's productivity.

Nitrogen is a crucial element for plant growth as it is necessary for the formation of proteins and chlorophyll, which are essential components of plant cells. Nitrogen is also an important element for the growth of leaves and plant stems. Plants that lack nitrogen often have yellow leaves and delayed growth. Sources of nitrogen include organic fertilizers such as manure, compost, and plant waste, as well as mineral fertilizers such as potassium nitrate and urea.

Phosphorus is essential for the growth and development of plant roots, as well as for fruit and seed production. Phosphorus is also important for energy transfer in plant cells. Plants that lack phosphorus often have underdeveloped roots and slow growth. Sources of phosphorus include organic fertilizers such as crushed bones and wood ashes, as well as mineral fertilizers such as superphosphate.

Potassium is necessary for overall plant growth and the production of high-quality fruits and vegetables. Potassium also helps plants resist diseases and environmental stresses such as drought and cold. Plants that lack potassium often have yellow, wilted, or burnt edges on their leaves. Sources of potassium include organic fertilizers such as wood ashes and seaweed, as well as mineral fertilizers such as potassium sulfate and potash.

It is important to note that maintaining a balance of macronutrients is essential for optimal plant growth. An excess or deficiency of any nutrient can cause damage to plants and affect their productivity. Therefore, it is important to test the soil to determine macronutrient levels and adjust inputs accordingly.

Micronutrients and their role in plant growth

Micronutrients are essential elements for plant growth, even though they are required in small quantities. Their absence or deficiency can cause growth and development problems in plants, which manifest as visible symptoms such as yellow leaves or weak and fragile stems.

Calcium is essential for root growth and cell wall formation. It also helps regulate soil pH and improve nutrient absorption by plants. Sources of calcium include lime, dolomite, and crushed eggshells.

Magnesium is an important component of chlorophyll, the molecule responsible for photosynthesis. It is therefore vital for leaf growth and food production for the plant. Sources of magnesium include dolomite, epsomite, and Epsom salts.

Sulfur is a key element in the formation of proteins, amino acids, and vitamins. It is also important for the production of essential oils and pigments in plants. Sources of sulfur include sulfur powder, magnesium sulfate, and iron sulfate.

Iron is essential for the production of chlorophyll and the absorption of other nutrients such as nitrogen. Plants can suffer from iron deficiencies if the soil is too alkaline or if the roots cannot absorb enough nutrients. Sources of iron include iron sulfate and chelated amino acids.

Manganese is an important element for photosynthesis and chlorophyll production. It also plays a role in soil pH regulation. Manganese deficiencies can result in leaf diseases and symptoms similar to iron deficiency. Sources of manganese include manganese sulfate and chelated amino acids.

Copper is necessary for chlorophyll production and disease resistance. Plants can suffer from copper deficiencies in alkaline soils or when the pH is imbalanced. Sources of copper include copper sulfate and chelated amino acids.

Zinc is essential for root growth and the production of growth hormones. It also helps regulate water consumption by plants. Zinc deficiencies can cause growth problems and symptoms similar to iron deficiency. Sources of zinc include zinc sulfate and chelated amino acids.

Boron is an important element for root growth and cellulose production. Boron deficiencies can result in growth deformities and reproductive problems in plants. Sources of boron include sodium borate and boron sulfate.

Molybdenum is necessary for the production of certain enzymes that are important for nitrogen fixation in plants. Molybdenum deficiencies can cause growth problems and symptoms similar to nitrogen deficiency. Sources of molybdenum include sodium molybdate and ammonium molybdate.

It is important to note that most soils naturally contain sufficient amounts of micronutrients for plants. However, there may be cases where plants suffer from deficiencies due to factors such as soil pH, climatic conditions, or irrigation water quality. In these cases, applying appropriate amendments can help correct micronutrient deficiencies.

It is also important to note that the balance of micronutrients is essential for optimal plant growth. Deficiencies or excesses of certain micronutrients can affect the absorption and utilization of other nutrients. Therefore, it is important to closely monitor micronutrient levels in the soil and correct any imbalances.

The importance of nutrient balance

Maintaining a balanced nutrient profile in the soil is crucial for optimal garden productivity. Plants require various types of nutrients for their growth, including macronutrients such as nitrogen, phosphorus, and potassium, as well as micronutrients such as calcium, magnesium, sulfur, iron, manganese, copper, zinc, boron, and molybdenum.

All of these nutrients must be present in balanced proportions for plants to efficiently absorb them. A deficiency in any single nutrient can affect plant growth and yield, while nutrient excess can result in over-fertilization and environmental problems such as water pollution.

Soil pH also influences nutrient availability for plants. pH levels that are too high or too low can make certain nutrients inaccessible to plants, leading to nutritional deficiencies.

To maintain nutrient balance in the soil, it is important to practice crop rotation and add organic and mineral amendments based on soil analysis results. Organic amendments such as compost, manure, and cover crops can improve soil organic matter and nutrient content, while mineral amendments can adjust pH and correct nutrient deficiencies.

It is also important to monitor the quality of irrigation water and avoid excessive use of chemical fertilizers to prevent excessive nutrient levels in the soil.

Soil pH and its influence on nutrient availability

Soil pH is a key factor in soil fertility and nutrient availability for plants. pH measures the acidity or alkalinity of the soil on a scale ranging from 0 to 14, with 7 being neutral. pH below 7 is considered acidic, while pH above 7 is alkaline.

Soil pH has a significant influence on the solubility of nutrients in the soil. Nutrients required for plant growth are soluble in water at specific pH ranges. For example, phosphorus is more available at a slightly acidic pH between 6 and 7, whereas nitrogen is more available at a slightly alkaline pH between 7 and 8.

An excessively acidic or alkaline pH can also affect plant growth. A soil that is too acidic can make certain nutrients toxic to plants and limit their growth. Conversely, a soil that is too alkaline can limit nutrient availability and result in nutritional deficiencies in plants.

Therefore, maintaining an optimal soil pH is important to maximize your garden's productivity. Soil pH can be adjusted by adding specific amendments such as limestone to raise pH or sulfur to lower pH.

It is important to note that the addition of amendments to adjust soil pH should be done carefully and based on soil analysis results to avoid overcorrection mistakes. Regular soil analysis is therefore important to monitor soil pH and ensure nutrient availability for plants.

In summary, soil pH is a key factor in soil fertility and nutrient availability for plants. It is important to maintain optimal soil pH to maximize your garden's productivity. Adding amendments to adjust soil pH should be done carefully and based on soil analysis results...

Soil Analysis and Interpretation

Soil Sampling Methods

Soil sampling is a crucial step in soil fertility management. The obtained results can help identify nutrient needs and deficiencies, determine pH levels, organic matter content, soil structure, etc. Once the results are known, it is possible to implement appropriate amendments and cultivation techniques to maximize garden productivity.

There are several methods for soil sampling. The most common method involves taking samples at various depths using an auger or a shovel. The collected samples must be representative of the area to be analyzed. It is important to take samples from multiple locations in the garden to have a comprehensive view of soil fertility.

The number of samples to be taken depends on the size of the area to be analyzed. Generally, it is recommended to take one sample for every 500 to 1000 square meters. It is also advisable to take samples at different times of the year, preferably in autumn or spring, when soil conditions are stable.

The collected samples should be thoroughly mixed to obtain a homogeneous sample. A small amount of this mixture can then be taken and sent to the laboratory for analysis. Laboratories may use different analysis methods to measure nutrient content, pH levels, organic matter, etc.

Choosing a reliable laboratory for soil analysis is important. Laboratories must adhere to strict standards and use recognized analysis methods to ensure the reliability of the results. The obtained results must be interpreted carefully to implement appropriate amendments and cultivation techniques.

Soil Testing and its Results

Soil analysis is an essential process for any gardener who wants to maximize garden productivity. It helps understand soil characteristics, available nutrients for plants, and necessary amendments to improve soil quality.

Soil tests provide valuable information on soil pH, nutrient levels, and physical properties. Tests can be performed using soil testing kits available in gardening stores or by sending soil samples to specialized laboratories.

Soil testing kits are easy to use and provide quick and affordable results. They are useful for amateur gardeners who want to get a general idea of their soil's characteristics. The results can indicate soil pH, nutrient levels such as nitrogen, phosphorus, and potassium, as well as soil texture.

Specialized laboratories provide more detailed soil analyses. The results include a comprehensive analysis of soil quality, including pH levels, nutrient levels, soil texture, organic matter content, and the presence of toxic elements such as lead and cadmium. Laboratories can also provide recommendations for amendments to improve soil quality.

The results of soil tests must be properly interpreted to make informed decisions on the necessary amendments to improve soil quality. Gardeners need to understand the limitations and advantages of each type of soil test and be able to address the problems identified by soil analysis.

Understanding Soil Analysis Results

Soil analysis is a crucial step for any gardener who wants to improve soil fertility and maximize garden productivity. However, analysis results may seem complex and difficult to interpret for an amateur gardener. In this section, we will explore the different key elements to consider when analyzing soil analysis results.

First and foremost, it is important to know that soil analysis results provide information on soil nutrient elements and physical properties. These results allow you to determine the nutrients and amendments your soil needs to improve its fertility. The analysis results can also provide indications on soil texture, pH, and other important physical properties.

When analyzing soil analysis results, the first thing to consider is soil pH. pH is a measure of soil acidity or alkalinity. Neutral pH is 7.0, below which the soil is acidic, and above which it is alkaline. Soil pH is important because it affects nutrient availability for plants. Plants require a soil pH suitable for their type and nutrient needs to be able to absorb the necessary nutrients for their growth.

Next, soil analysis results provide information on the levels of different essential nutrient elements, such as nitrogen, phosphorus, and potassium. The levels of these elements are important as they influence plant growth and development. Analysis results can also indicate levels of micronutrients such as calcium, magnesium, sulfur, and other nutrients that are also important for plants.

In addition to nutrient levels, soil analysis results can also provide information on other important physical properties of the soil, such as soil texture, moisture content, and water retention capacity. These physical properties are important as they influence plant health and growth.

Once you understand soil analysis results, you can determine the necessary amendments to improve soil fertility. Amendments may include organic or mineral fertilizers, organic matter, pH correctors, or other specific amendments depending on your soil's needs. It is important to choose the right amendments to avoid excess nutrient inputs or worsening pH problems.

Finally, it is important to understand that soil analysis results are just a reference tool and that regular monitoring of your soil's health is important to ensure your plants receive the necessary nutrients. Soil health can also be improved through proper management practices such as crop rotation, cover cropping, mulching, composting, and efficient irrigation.

Natural Amendments and Fertilizers

Soil Amendment to Correct pH and Nutrient Deficiencies

Soil amendment is a key element in correcting nutrient deficiencies and adjusting soil pH to maximize garden productivity. Plants need certain nutrients to grow and thrive, and these nutrients must be present in the soil in sufficient quantities and balanced proportions to enable optimal growth.

Amendments can be classified into two categories: organic amendments and mineral amendments. Organic amendments include materials such as manure, compost, leaf litter, and crop residues. They improve soil structure and provide nutrients slowly but steadily to plants. Mineral amendments include materials such as limestone, magnesium sulfate, and mineral fertilizers. They provide nutrients quickly to plants, but excessive use can disrupt the nutrient balance in the soil.

Before adding amendments to the soil, it is important to understand the needs of your plants and the characteristics of your soil. You can obtain information about the composition of your soil by conducting a soil analysis. This analysis will provide you with information about nutrient levels, pH, and other important soil characteristics.

Once you have understood the needs of your plants and the characteristics of your soil, you can start adding amendments to correct nutrient deficiencies and adjust pH. Organic amendments are an excellent way to add nutrients and improve soil structure, while mineral amendments can be used to correct nutrient imbalances and adjust pH.

When choosing amendments, it is important to consider the needs of your plants and the characteristics of your soil. For example, if you have clay soil, you can use organic amendments to improve soil structure and allow better drainage. If your soil is acidic, you can use limestone to adjust pH.

Different Categories of Amendments

In gardening practice, amendments are organic or mineral materials that are added to the soil to improve its quality and fertility. There are several categories of amendments, each with unique properties and specific benefits for the soil and plants.

The first category of amendments is organic matter. This includes compost, manure, straw, leaf litter, and other organic waste. Organic matter is important because it improves soil texture, increases the soil's water and nutrient retention capacity, and promotes the growth of beneficial microorganisms in the soil. Compost is an excellent amendment because it is rich in nutrients, easy to produce and apply, and a great way to recycle organic waste.

The second category of amendments is lime and minerals. Lime is used to adjust soil pH, especially for acidic soils. Minerals such as magnesium sulfate, potassium sulfate, and natural phosphate are used to provide essential nutrients to plants and improve soil fertility. Minerals can also help improve soil structure and prevent nutrient deficiencies.

The third category of amendments is commercial products such as organic and mineral fertilizers. Organic fertilizers such as guano, blood and bone meal, manure, and seaweed are derived from natural sources and are often slower to decompose and release nutrients into the soil. Mineral fertilizers are made from mineral sources and are often faster to release nutrients into the soil.

The fourth category of amendments is natural products such as charcoal, perlite, vermiculite, and sand. These amendments are often used to improve soil structure, enhance water retention, and help prevent soil compaction.

Lastly, the final category of amendments is bioactivators such as mycorrhizae and nitrogen-fixing bacteria. These amendments are used to enhance plant growth, stimulate nutrient production in the soil, and promote soil health. Mycorrhizae are fungi that colonize plant roots and help increase their nutrient and water absorption capacity. Nitrogen-fixing bacteria are beneficial microorganisms that help convert atmospheric nitrogen into a form that plants can use.

How to Adapt Amendments Based on Soil Analysis Results

To maximize garden productivity, it is essential to adapt amendments based on soil analysis results. Soil analysis will help you determine which nutrients your soil is lacking and the necessary amendments to correct these deficiencies.

Amendments are substances added to the soil to improve its structure, texture, and composition. There are different categories such as organic amendments, mineral amendments, and biological amendments.

It is important to choose the right amendments to correct nutrient deficiencies in your soil. Organic amendments such as compost, manure, and crop residues provide nutrients and organic matter to the soil. Mineral amendments such as limestone, phosphate, and magnesium sulfate provide nutrients in a readily available form for plants. Biological amendments such as mycorrhizae and nitrogen-fixing bacteria promote plant growth by enhancing soil health.

Adapting amendments based on soil analysis results is a crucial step for effective amendment use. If your soil is acidic, you can add limestone to increase pH. If your soil is low in nitrogen, you can add nitrogen-rich amendments such as manure or nitrogen-rich crop residues. If your soil is low in phosphorus, you can add phosphate.

It is also important not to add too many amendments, as this can lead to nutrient accumulation in the soil and disrupt the natural balance of the soil. Excessive amendments can also make nutrients less available to plants.

Lastly, regular soil analysis is important to monitor changes in soil composition and adjust amendments accordingly. Adapting amendments based on soil analysis results is a crucial step to maximize soil fertility and garden productivity.

The Importance of Organic Matter in the Soil

Organic matter is a key element for soil fertility. It comes from plant and animal debris that naturally decompose in the soil, providing essential nutrients for plant growth. It also plays an important role in the development of beneficial microorganisms that live in the soil and contribute to plant health.

The importance of organic matter is not limited to providing nutrients for plants, but it also helps regulate soil moisture. Soils rich in organic matter can retain water for longer, allowing plants to better withstand drought.

Organic matter can also help regulate soil temperature. Soils rich in organic matter can retain heat for longer, which can help protect plant roots from extreme temperatures.

It is important to note that the amount of organic matter in the soil can vary significantly depending on the soil type and land management practices used. Intensive agricultural practices such as excessive use of pesticides and chemical fertilizers can significantly reduce the amount of organic matter in the soil. This can have a negative impact on plant health and long-term soil quality.

To maximize the amount of organic matter in the soil, it is important to practice sustainable agricultural techniques. This can include using manure, compost, and other organic amendments to add nutrients and organic matter to the soil. Cover cropping and crop rotation can also help increase the amount of organic matter in the soil by reducing erosion and adding nutrients to the soil.

Organic Fertilizers: Manure, Compost, Guano, etc.

Organic fertilizers are natural amendments that can significantly improve soil fertility. They are derived from organic materials such as manure, compost, guano, crop residues, etc. These organic fertilizers are sources of essential nutrients for plants, but their use must be tailored to the specific needs of the soil and plants.

Manure is a commonly used organic fertilizer. It is composed of animal feces and urine mixed with straw, sawdust, or other plant materials. Manure can be used fresh or composted. However, the use of fresh manure can cause health problems for plants and encourage weed proliferation. Manure must be properly composted before use to avoid these issues.

Compost is another popular organic fertilizer. It is made from organic materials such as leaves, grass clippings, vegetable and fruit scraps, etc. Composting is a process of decomposing organic materials by microorganisms, which produces a nutrient-rich amendment. Composting must be done correctly to avoid problems with bad odors and bacterial contamination.

Guano is an organic fertilizer of animal origin made up of bird droppings. It is rich in nutrients such as nitrogen, phosphorus, potassium, and trace elements. Guano is usually used in small quantities due to its high concentration.

Crop residues, such as straw and husks, can also be used as organic fertilizers. They are rich in organic matter and can improve soil structure by aerating it and making it more permeable to water and air.

The use of organic fertilizers has several advantages. They are more cost-effective than mineral fertilizers and are often available for free. Organic fertilizers also improve soil quality by increasing its organic matter and beneficial microorganism content. They also reduce the risk of environmental pollution and protect the health of plants and animals.

However, the use of organic fertilizers must be done with caution. Overuse can lead to soil and groundwater contamination issues. It is therefore important to follow recommended organic fertilizer application guidelines and have a thorough understanding of the needs of the soil and plants.

Mineral Fertilizers: Limestone, Magnesium Sulfate, etc.

Mineral fertilizers are substances that contain essential plant nutrients such as nitrogen, phosphorus, potassium, calcium, magnesium, sulfur, and other trace elements. These elements are extracted from natural sources such as mines or quarries and then processed into products that can be readily used by plants.

Limestone is a commonly used mineral fertilizer to correct soil acidity. It is primarily composed of calcium carbonate and can be applied in the form of quicklime, hydrated lime, or dolomite. When applied to the soil, limestone reacts with soil acidity to form calcium and carbon dioxide, thereby increasing soil pH and improving nutrient availability to plants. However, it is important not to apply too much limestone, as it can make the soil too alkaline and result in trace element deficiencies.

Magnesium sulfate is another commonly used mineral fertilizer to enrich the soil with magnesium. Magnesium is an essential nutrient for plants as it is involved in many important biochemical reactions for growth and development. Magnesium sulfate is also used to correct sulfur deficiencies in the soil.

While mineral fertilizers can be effective in improving soil fertility, it is important to understand that excessive use can have adverse effects on the environment and plant health. The use of mineral fertilizers can lead to salt accumulation in the soil, which can render the soil sterile in the long term.

Additionally, excessive use of nitrogen can cause foliar burns and make plants more susceptible to diseases and pests.

Therefore, it is important to have a good understanding of the needs of your plants and soil before using mineral fertilizers. It is recommended to conduct a soil analysis to determine nutrient deficiencies and tailor mineral fertilizer use accordingly. Additionally, using organic fertilizers such as compost, manure, and green manure cover crops is recommended to improve soil fertility in a sustainable and environmentally friendly manner.

Improving Soil Fertility Naturally

The Composting Process and Best Composting Practices

Composting is a process of transforming organic waste into a nutrient-rich soil amendment for plants. It is a sustainable and cost-effective method to improve soil fertility and reduce household waste.

The composting process begins with collecting organic materials such as food scraps, dead leaves, and garden debris. These waste materials are then placed in a composter or compost pile. It is important to balance carbon-rich and nitrogen-rich materials to ensure fast and efficient decomposition.

Carbon-rich materials like dead leaves and branches provide the necessary structure and airflow for composting, while nitrogen-rich materials like food scraps and garden debris supply the nutrients needed by the microorganisms that break down the compost.

Composting requires proper management to avoid issues such as bad odors, flies, and rodents. It is crucial to keep the compost pile moist but not overly wet, add dry materials to prevent excessive moisture, and turn the pile regularly to ensure proper aeration.

Best composting practices also include adding compost

activators to stimulate the growth of microorganisms and accelerate the decomposition process. Examples of compost activators include mature compost, manure, cow dung, seaweed, and crushed eggshells.

Compost is ready to be used when the materials have fully decomposed into a dark brown, crumbly, and odorless soil amendment. Compost can be used to enrich the soil, improve soil structure, reduce erosion, retain moisture, and promote plant growth.

Composting is a simple and effective method to improve soil fertility and reduce household waste. By adopting best composting practices, amateur gardeners can produce nutrient-rich soil amendments for their plants and contribute to environmental preservation.

Cover Crops and Green Manure

Cover crops and green manure are ecological agricultural practices that involve growing specific plants to improve soil quality and fertility. Cover crops and green manure have numerous benefits for soil, plants, and the environment.

Cover crops are crops planted to enrich the soil with nutrients. Cover crops can be legumes like clover, lupine, pea, or beans, or grasses like rye, oats, vetch, etc. Green manure crops are plants grown to cover the soil and improve its structure. Green manure crops can be legumes or grasses.

The advantages of cover crops and green manure are

manifold. Firstly, these plants add organic matter to the soil, enhancing its structure and water retention capacity. Additionally, plant roots help aerate the soil, prevent erosion, and improve soil biodiversity by providing food and habitat for soil organisms.

Furthermore, cover crops and green manure can help reduce weed growth by competing for nutrients and space with undesirable plants. They can also aid in reducing damage caused by diseases and insects by attracting natural predators of pests and boosting plant resistance.

Cover crops and green manure can also help increase soil nitrogen content. Legumes, in particular, have the ability to fix nitrogen from the air into the soil, reducing the need for expensive synthetic nitrogen fertilizers.

It is important to choose cover crops and green manure that are best suited for your soil and climate. Legumes are often used to add nitrogen to the soil, while grasses are commonly used to improve soil structure. Winter cover crops can help protect the soil from erosion and reduce nutrient loss.

Additionally, selecting plant species that best align with your gardening goals is crucial. For example, some plants may be better suited for combating soil diseases or attracting natural insect predators.

Finally, understanding when and how to plant cover crops and green manure is essential in maximizing their benefits for the soil and plants. Cover crops and green manure can be planted simultaneously with main crops or between crops to cover the soil between harvests.

The Benefits of Cover Crops

Cover crops are a sustainable soil management technique that involves planting temporary crops on fallow land. These cover crops are either left on the land to naturally decompose or incorporated into the soil to enhance its structure and fertility. This technique offers multiple advantages for gardeners and farmers.

Firstly, cover crops help protect the soil from erosion and nutrient depletion. The plant roots stabilize the soil, preventing erosion from water and wind. Moreover, cover crops are rich in organic matter, which nourishes soil microorganisms and improves its structure. Cover crops also help suppress weeds by occupying space and preventing their growth.

Secondly, cover crops have a positive impact on soil biodiversity. Plant roots attract soil organisms such as earthworms, bacteria, and fungi, which contribute to humus formation and the fixation of atmospheric nitrogen. Cover crops promote soil microbial life and enhance fertility.

Additionally, cover crops are an effective water management technique. Plant roots retain water in the soil and reduce evaporation. Cover crops thus help preserve moisture in the soil, which is particularly important in arid regions or areas prone to drought.

Lastly, cover crops can be used to improve soil quality and combat plant diseases. Some cover crops, like legumes, fix atmospheric nitrogen in the soil, reducing the need for synthetic chemical fertilizers while enhancing soil quality. Other cover crops, like mustards, have antifungal properties and can be used to combat plant diseases.

The Use of Mycorrhizae and Nitrogen-Fixing Bacteria

The use of mycorrhizae and nitrogen-fixing bacteria is a technique increasingly employed by gardeners to enhance soil fertility. Mycorrhizae are fungi that form a symbiotic relationship with plant roots, exchanging nutrients with them. Nitrogen-fixing bacteria, on the other hand, are microorganisms that live in the soil and have the ability to convert atmospheric nitrogen into a form usable by plants.

The utilization of mycorrhizae and nitrogen-fixing bacteria offers several benefits for gardeners. Firstly, these microorganisms improve soil structure by making it more aerated and porous, thus promoting the development of plant roots. Additionally, mycorrhizae and nitrogen-fixing bacteria enhance soil quality by providing nutrients to plants, including increased availability of nitrogen, phosphorus, and potassium.

To use mycorrhizae and nitrogen-fixing bacteria in your garden, you can purchase them in powder or granular form from gardening stores. It is also possible to naturally obtain them by using well-decomposed compost or manure, which naturally contain these microorganisms.

To apply mycorrhizae and nitrogen-fixing bacteria in your garden, you can mix them with compost or manure before spreading them on your soil. It is important to follow the instructions provided with the product you have purchased, as the recommended usage amounts may vary depending on the size of your garden and the type of soil you have.

Soil Fertility Improvement Techniques

Crop Rotation and Companion Planting

Crop rotation and companion planting are essential practices for maintaining soil fertility and maximizing garden productivity. Crop rotation involves alternating different types of crops in the same location to avoid soil depletion and limit the spread of diseases and pests. Companion planting, on the other hand, involves cultivating different plant species together in the same plot based on their compatibility and complementarity.

Crop rotation can be implemented according to various patterns, but the general idea is to avoid growing the same crop in the same place for several consecutive years. For example, if tomatoes are grown in a garden plot this year, it is preferable to plant beans or zucchini in the same plot the following year. This helps reduce the pressure of pests and diseases specific to tomatoes, while allowing the soil to regenerate with new nutrients.

Companion planting is a method that involves planting different plant species together to maximize their growth and resistance to pests and diseases. This technique is based on the principle that certain plants have beneficial relationships with each other, while others may compete or hinder one another. For example, beans have the ability to fix nitrogen in the soil, while squash has broad leaves that help protect the soil from excessive water evaporation. By planting these two species together, a beneficial symbiosis is created for both plants.

It is important to plan crop rotation and companion planting based on the season, climate, and soil characteristics. Some plants prefer more acidic or alkaline soil, while others need more water or sunlight. By carefully planning these practices, we can maximize the benefits for both plants and the soil.

Soil Management: Tillage, Aeration, Mulching

Soil management is an essential practice for maintaining the fertility of your garden and maximizing crop productivity. A well-managed soil allows plants to better absorb the nutrients, water, and air necessary for their growth.

However, there are different methods of soil management, each with its advantages and disadvantages. Here, we will focus on the three main techniques: tillage, aeration, and mulching.

Tillage is a traditional method that involves deeply turning the soil with a spade or plow. This practice helps loosen and aerate the soil, making it easier to work with. However, tillage can also have negative effects on soil quality by disrupting the biological balance and exposing nutrients to the air, leading to fertility loss. Additionally, tillage requires a lot of physical effort, time, and energy.

To overcome these drawbacks, there is a more sustainable and effective alternative: soil aeration. This technique involves creating holes in the soil using a digging fork, manual or mechanical aerator, or even letting plant roots do the work. Aeration promotes the growth of roots and beneficial microorganisms, facilitates water and air circulation in the soil, and limits the spread of diseases and pests.

Mulching is another soil management method that involves covering the soil surface with a layer of organic matter such as straw, dead leaves, grass clippings, wood chips, or compost. This cover helps retain soil moisture, regulate temperature, suppress weed growth, and nourish the soil with organic matter. Mulching can also enhance biodiversity by providing habitat for beneficial insects and microorganisms.

However, it is important to choose the appropriate mulch for your plants and soil. Too dense of a mulch can prevent seeds from germinating, while too light of a mulch can be carried away by wind or rain. Additionally, mulch needs to be replenished regularly to maintain its effectiveness.

In summary, soil management is a key practice to maximize the productivity of your garden. Tillage can be replaced by more sustainable and effective techniques such as soil aeration and mulching. By adopting these methods, you can improve the quality of your soil and promote the growth of healthy and productive plants.

Agroforestry and Intercropping

Agroforestry is a cultivation technique that involves combining trees and crops on the same piece of land. It is a method that can contribute to the creation of fertile soil and increase garden productivity. Trees provide protection against wind and sunlight, as well as support for climbing crops. Additionally, their roots help maintain soil integrity and improve its structure.

Intercropping is another technique that can be used in conjunction with agroforestry. This technique involves growing secondary crops that are compatible with the main crops between rows. Intercropping can have multiple benefits, such as nitrogen fixation, weed control, soil quality improvement, and water loss reduction.

Agroforestry and intercropping can be employed in various types of gardens, including vegetable gardens, community gardens, and urban farms. They can be used to cultivate a variety of plants, including vegetables, fruits, herbs, and ornamental plants.

It is important to note that agroforestry and intercropping require careful planning and proper implementation. Trees should be planted at an appropriate distance from the crops to avoid competition for water and nutrients. Additionally, intercropped crops must be carefully selected to avoid resource competition between the main crops and intercrops.

By effectively utilizing agroforestry and intercropping, gardeners can improve soil fertility, increase garden productivity, and reduce production costs. These techniques can also contribute to environmental conservation by reducing the use of chemicals and preserving biodiversity.

The Role of Plants in Soil Fertility

Nitrogen-Fixing Plants

Nitrogen-fixing plants are capable of converting atmospheric nitrogen into a form that is usable by other plants. This ability is due to a symbiotic relationship with bacteria called Rhizobia. Rhizobia live in the root nodules of nitrogen-fixing plants, where they convert atmospheric nitrogen into ammonium, a nitrogen compound that plants can absorb and use for growth.

Nitrogen-fixing plants are particularly beneficial in gardens and crops as they improve soil fertility by providing nitrogen to neighboring plants. They are also environmentally friendly as they reduce the need for synthetic nitrogen fertilizers in crop cultivation.

There are numerous nitrogen-fixing plants, including legumes such as beans, peas, broad beans, lentils, and clovers. Legumes are often used as cover crops to enrich the soil with nitrogen before planting vegetables or fruits. Cover crops of legumes can also be used to enhance soil fertility in preparation for the next season.

It is important to note that not all legumes are nitrogen-fixing plants, so it is crucial to choose the right varieties to reap maximum benefits. For example, some clover varieties are better nitrogen fixers than others.

In addition to legumes, there are also other nitrogen-fixing plants such as trees, shrubs, and perennials. Trees like acacia, mimosa, and locust are often used to improve the fertility of poor soils. Shrubs like blackcurrant, redcurrant, and elderberry are also common nitrogen fixers in gardens. Perennial plants like alfalfa, fern, and vetch are also popular choices for enhancing soil fertility.

Lastly, it is important to note that nitrogen-fixing plants are not a miracle solution for all soil fertility problems. It is crucial to implement a comprehensive soil improvement strategy, which includes practices such as crop rotation, adding organic matter, and managing irrigation. However, the use of nitrogen-fixing plants can certainly contribute to improving soil fertility and maximizing garden productivity.

Soil-Loosening and Soil-Improving Plants

Soil-loosening and soil-improving plants are valuable allies for gardeners who want to enhance soil fertility naturally and sustainably. Soil-loosening plants are species that have the ability to break up compacted soil, allowing air, water, and nutrients to circulate more effectively. Soil-improving plants, on the other hand, are plants that can capture and fix atmospheric nitrogen through their roots, thus increasing the soil's nitrogen content.

Among soil-loosening plants, we can mention radish, white clover, rye, and mustard. These plants have deep roots that can penetrate the soil, breaking up its compacted structure and promoting the circulation of water, air, and nutrients. Moreover, these plants can be used as green manure, as when they are crushed and incorporated into the soil, they enrich it with organic matter and nutrients.

Soil-improving plants include legumes such as beans, peas, broad beans, alfalfa, and clovers. These plants have symbiotic bacteria in their roots that enable them to fix atmospheric nitrogen and make it available to other plants in the garden. Additionally, legumes have roots that promote soil structure and microbial activity, thereby improving overall soil fertility.

In addition to enhancing soil structure and fertility, soil-loosening and soil-improving plants can also contribute to disease and pest prevention. For example, white clover can repel nematodes, while mustard can be used as a natural fungicide.

It is important to choose the right soil-loosening and soil-improving plants for your garden based on your soil and climate conditions. It is also important to plant them at the right time of year and incorporate them properly into the soil.

Soil Quality Indicator Plants

When it comes to growing plants, understanding the quality of the soil they will be planted in is crucial. Soil quality indicator plants can help gardeners assess the quality of their soil. These plants have specific soil requirements and can therefore indicate the quality and characteristics of the soil they grow in.

Some soil quality indicator plants indicate nitrogen-rich soil, such as legumes like beans or peas. Legumes have a symbiotic relationship with nitrogen-fixing bacteria that allow them to absorb nitrogen from the air and convert it into a plant-usable nutrient.

Other soil quality indicator plants, like clovers, indicate acidic soil, while plants that prefer alkaline soils, such as asparagus, may indicate higher pH levels.

Soil quality indicator plants can also indicate physical characteristics of the soil, such as its structure and texture. For example, plants that thrive in sandy and well-drained soil may indicate that the soil is light and permeable, while plants that thrive in clayey and dense soil may indicate that the soil is heavier and retains more water.

By observing the plants that naturally grow in a garden, gardeners can learn a lot about their soil and adapt their cultivation accordingly. Soil quality indicator plants can also help identify areas of the garden that require specific amendments or care.

It is important to note that soil quality indicator plants only provide an indication of soil quality, and other factors can influence plant growth. Therefore, it is important to combine observation of soil quality indicator plants with other soil analysis techniques, such as soil testing and pH tests, to obtain a more comprehensive picture of soil quality.

Advanced Techniques to Maximize Garden Productivity

Permaculture and Its Basic Principles

Permaculture is a sustainable agricultural system that aims to create a productive and self-sufficient ecosystem. It is based on a set of principles and practices inspired by nature to produce food and resources while preserving the environment. In other words, permaculture involves imitating nature to achieve sustainable production.

Permaculture principles are based on the philosophy of sustainability and understanding the interactions between elements in a system. These principles include diversity, cooperation, autonomy, efficiency, self-regulation, and regeneration.

Diversity is essential in permaculture as it optimizes system productivity and resilience. By using a wide variety of plants, animals, and microorganisms, the system becomes more resistant to diseases and pests, and can adapt to environmental changes.

Cooperation is also important in permaculture as it maximizes positive interactions between system elements. For example, plants can be chosen based on their ability to support each other by providing nutrients or shade.

Autonomy is another key principle of permaculture as it

reduces dependency on external resources. Permaculture systems are designed to be self-sufficient, using local resources and recycling waste to create new products.

Efficiency is also important in permaculture as it maximizes production with minimal effort and resources. Permaculture systems are designed to be efficient, using appropriate cultivation methods and reducing losses.

Self-regulation is another important principle in permaculture as it maintains balance in the system. Permaculture systems are designed to be self-regulating, utilizing appropriate cultivation techniques and minimizing disturbances.

Lastly, regeneration is a key principle of permaculture as it restores soil fertility and the environment. Permaculture systems are designed to be regenerative, using appropriate cultivation methods and promoting plant growth and reproduction.

Permaculture can be applied to various scales, from household gardens to commercial farms. Permaculture practices include guild planting (groups of mutually supportive plants), raised-bed gardening, waste management and compost production, using animals for fertilizer and food production, and water conservation.

By embracing permaculture principles, gardeners can create productive and sustainable gardens while preserving the environment. By imitating nature, permaculture systems can be more resilient, self-sufficient, and regenerative compared to conventional agricultural systems. They can also offer environmental benefits such as soil conservation, reduced greenhouse gas emissions, and biodiversity restoration.

Aquaponics and Hydroponic Cultivation

Aquaponics and hydroponics are innovative cultivation methods that can be used to maximize garden productivity while minimizing water and fertilizer consumption, and producing healthier and more nutritious crops.

Aquaponics is an integrated cultivation system that combines plant cultivation with fish farming. The basic principle is simple: fish provide nutrients to the plants, while the plants purify the water for the fish. The plants are grown in water-filled tanks that circulate through the system, absorbing nutrients from the fish. This nutrient-enriched water is then returned to the fish tanks, creating a closed and balanced cycle.

On the other hand, hydroponic cultivation is a method of growing plants without soil. The plants are grown in an inert growing medium such as rockwool or perlite, and receive the necessary nutrients through a nutrient solution that circulates in the system. This cultivation method allows for easier control of nutrients, water, and the environment in which plants grow, greatly improving garden productivity.

There are numerous advantages to aquaponics and hydroponics. Firstly, these cultivation methods use much less water compared to traditional methods, which is particularly important in areas where water is scarce or expensive. Additionally, these cultivation methods allow for easier control of nutrients and environmental conditions, resulting in improved plant growth and health. Lastly, these methods can be used to produce crops year-round, which is particularly advantageous in areas with short growing seasons.

However, it should be noted that setting up aquaponics and hydroponics systems can be more costly compared to traditional cultivation methods. Additionally, these cultivation methods require constant monitoring to maintain a healthy balance between fish, plants, and water.

In conclusion, aquaponics and hydroponics are innovative cultivation methods that can be used to maximize garden productivity.

Biodynamics and the Use of Biodynamic Preparations

Biodynamics is an alternative agricultural method that aims to cultivate high-quality food while respecting the environment and restoring the natural balance of soils. This method is based on the idea that soil, plants, and animals are all interconnected and interdependent, and that by treating the soil holistically, the health of plants, animals, and humans consuming their products can be improved.

One of the most well-known practices in biodynamics is the use of biodynamic preparations, which are blends of plants, minerals, and other natural substances that are dynamized to stimulate life in the soil and improve plant health. There are nine different preparations, which are used at specific times in the lunar cycle to maximize their effectiveness.

Biodynamic preparations are typically used in conjunction with other biodynamic practices such as crop rotation, green manure, and biodiversity conservation. These practices together aim to stimulate life in the soil, improve soil fertility, and create a healthy growing environment for plants.

While biodynamics is often considered an esoteric or mystical method, there is ample scientific evidence supporting its effectiveness. Studies have shown that biodynamic practices can increase nutrient content in food, improve soil health, and reduce damage caused by diseases and pests.

However, it is important to note that biodynamics may not be suitable for all types of crops and soils. Before implementing biodynamic practices in your garden, it is important to conduct a thorough analysis of your soil and choose practices that best suit your situation.

Ultimately, biodynamics is an alternative agricultural method that aims to cultivate high-quality food while respecting the environment and restoring the natural balance of soils. When used correctly, it can be an effective method for improving soil, plant, and overall environmental health.

Water and Irrigation Management

The Importance of Water in the Soil

Water is a crucial element for the health and productivity of the soil. Plants need water to absorb nutrients and maintain their cellular structure. Lack of water can cause significant damage to plant growth and survival.

However, excess water can also be harmful. Excess water can lead to the accumulation of harmful nutrients, such as salt, in the soil. It can also create an anaerobic environment that can kill beneficial microorganisms in the soil. Therefore, it is important to find a balance for irrigation and water management.

Proper water management in the soil involves understanding the water needs of different plants in the garden, as well as the optimal growing conditions. This may include observing local weather conditions and monitoring the amount of water that plants naturally receive through rainfall. Generally, plants need more water during periods of active growth, such as spring and summer, and less water during dormant periods in winter.

It is also important to understand the different irrigation techniques available and their impact on soil fertility. Drip irrigation can help preserve soil moisture by providing water directly to the plant roots. Sprinkler irrigation may be useful for watering larger areas, but it can result in water loss through evaporation and a reduction in soil fertility due to nutrient leaching.

Water conservation is also an important part of water management in the soil. This may include using mulch to retain moisture in the soil, collecting and reusing rainwater, and managing runoff water to prevent soil erosion.

Understanding Plant Water Needs

To understand plant water needs, it is essential to remember that water is a key element for plant growth and development. Plants require water for various reasons, including maintaining their structure, transporting nutrients, performing photosynthesis, and regulating temperature. Generally, plants need a regular water supply to maintain their health and productivity.

The amount of water required for plants depends on several factors, such as plant type, soil type, weather conditions, and cultivation practices. For example, plants grown in sandy soils require more water than those grown in clay soils. Plants growing under intense sunlight or in arid regions also require more water than those growing in temperate or humid areas.

It is important to understand that too much water can be as damaging to plants as too little. Excess water can lead to soil saturation, preventing plants from breathing and developing properly. It can also promote the proliferation of fungal diseases and pests that can damage roots and leaves.

To determine your plants' water needs, you can regularly monitor soil moisture using a hygrometer. This will help establish a regular watering schedule and adjust the frequency of watering according to your plants' specific needs. It is also important to consider local weather conditions, as periods of heavy rain or drought can affect your plants' water requirements.

Overall, understanding your plants' water needs is essential to maximize their productivity and health. By ensuring your plants receive an appropriate amount of water, you can help ensure their optimal growth and development. This can also help prevent diseases and pests that can harm your garden.

Different Irrigation Techniques and Their Impact on Soil Fertility

Irrigation is an important technique for ensuring healthy plant growth, but it can also impact soil fertility. Improper irrigation can result in nutrient loss and a decrease in soil quality. Therefore, it is important to be familiar with different irrigation techniques and their impact on soil fertility.

Sprinkler irrigation, where water is dispersed as fine droplets from pipes or sprinklers, is the most common irrigation method. While this technique effectively wets plants, it tends to waste water and disperse nutrients in the soil, which can reduce long-term fertility.

Drip irrigation is a more efficient alternative for saving water and preserving soil fertility. This technique delivers small amounts of water directly to plant roots through a system of emitters. Water is delivered slowly and deeply, reducing waste and allowing for more efficient nutrient utilization in the soil.

Another irrigation technique that can help preserve soil fertility is infiltration irrigation. This method allows water to gradually and deeply penetrate the soil, enabling better nutrient utilization. This technique requires permeable soils and may not be effective in clay soils or high precipitation areas.

It is also important to note that the quality of water used for irrigation can impact soil fertility. Salty or polluted waters can lead to salt accumulation in the soil, which can reduce fertility. Therefore, it is recommended to use quality water for irrigation and take measures to limit salt buildup in the soil.

Water Conservation and Resource Management

In this section, we will discuss water conservation and resource management, a crucial topic for maximizing soil fertility in your garden. Water is a precious and limited resource, and effective management is essential for maintaining soil and plant quality and quantity.

Firstly, it is important to understand your plants' water needs. Depending on the species, climate conditions, and soil type, water requirements may vary. Therefore, it is important to adjust irrigation based on these factors to avoid water waste and soil degradation. To assess your plants' water needs, you can use indicators such as leaf color, soil texture, evaporation rate, and climate.

Secondly, it is important to choose the appropriate irrigation method. There are several irrigation methods such as hand watering, sprinkler irrigation, drip irrigation, subsurface irrigation, etc. Each method has its advantages and disadvantages, but drip irrigation is considered the most effective and water-efficient method. It also helps maintain soil moisture consistently, which is beneficial for plants.

Furthermore, conserving water in your garden by avoiding unnecessary losses is important. You can recycle rainwater, for example, by using water collecting barrels. You can also use mulch to reduce water evaporation from the soil and maintain a constant soil temperature. Mulch also has other benefits, such as reducing weed growth and providing nutrients to the soil.

Finally, responsible and sustainable water resource management is important. It is recommended to plan your crops based on climate conditions and water availability, reduce water consumption by selecting climate-adapted plants, and avoiding unnecessary or excessive cultivation. You can also use automated irrigation systems that will help you save water and optimize your plant growth.

Drainage and Excess Water Management

Water management in a garden is crucial to ensure healthy and vigorous plant growth. However, excess water can quickly become a problem for soil fertility. Poor water management can lead to water-saturated soil, poor aeration, reduced oxygen content, nutrient loss, and proliferation of fungal diseases.

To avoid these problems, the first step is to assess your plants' water needs and adapt your irrigation system accordingly. It is important to regularly monitor the soil for signs of excess water, such as standing water, saturated surface, or yellowing leaves. If you notice these signs, it is time to take measures to improve your soil drainage.

One of the simplest solutions to improve drainage is to add organic matter to the soil. Organic matter, such as compost or manure, helps improve soil structure by creating air spaces and increasing water retention capacity. Organic matter also attracts beneficial microorganisms for soil health.

Another way to improve drainage is by adding sand or gravel to the soil. These materials create channels for water, allowing it to flow more easily through the soil. However, it is important not to add too much, as it can also result in nutrient loss.

Creating raised beds can also help improve drainage in gardens with clay or compacted soil. Raised beds allow water to flow more easily, reducing the risk of soil flooding.

Finally, a good practice is to install a drainage system in your garden. This system will drain excess water away from your garden, preventing flooding and drainage issues. It is important to plan the design of the drainage system to be effective and suitable for your garden's topography.

Prevention and Control of Pests, Diseases, and Soil Problems

The Enemies of the Soil

In the world of gardening, the enemies of the soil can take many forms, but some of the most common are nematodes and pathogenic fungi. Nematodes are microscopic worms that feed on plant roots and can cause considerable damage to crops. Pathogenic fungi, on the other hand, are microorganisms that can infect plants, cause diseases, and reduce yield.

Parasitic nematodes pose a serious threat to crops worldwide. They feed on plant roots, resulting in reduced growth and productivity. The most common nematodes are root-knot nematodes, which produce swellings on plant roots, cyst nematodes, which cause cyst formation on roots, and lesion nematodes, which damage plant roots and stems. Nematodes can be transmitted through soil, seeds, plants, tools, and even clothing.

Pathogenic fungi are also a danger to crops. Fungi can infect plants through roots, stems, leaves, or flowers. Symptoms vary depending on the plant and the disease but may include brown or black spots, wilted stems, yellow or spotted leaves, and fungi on the plant itself. Pathogenic fungi can survive in the soil and infect plants from year to year. Poor cultural practices, such as over-irrigation and over-fertilization, can promote the growth of pathogenic fungi.

To combat nematodes and pathogenic fungi, it is important to maintain a healthy and balanced soil. Cultural practices such as crop rotation, cover cropping, and composting can help improve soil health and reduce disease pressure. It is also important to use healthy seeds and monitor crops for signs of disease as soon as they appear. If a disease is identified, it is important to treat it promptly and appropriately to limit spread and minimize damage.

Techniques for Managing Soil Diseases and Pests

Soil diseases and pests can cause many problems for gardeners, leading to decreased productivity and even plant death. Fortunately, there are many techniques for managing these problems and maintaining a healthy and productive soil.

The first step in managing soil diseases and pests is prevention. It is important to maintain good garden hygiene by regularly removing dead leaves, plant debris, and weeds. This helps prevent the proliferation of pathogenic fungi and harmful insects. It is also important to choose plants that are resistant to local diseases and pests.

When diseases or pests are identified, it is important to treat them quickly before they spread. Biological treatments are often recommended for organic gardens as they do not contain harmful chemicals to the environment and humans. Examples of biological treatments include essential oils, baking soda, and insecticidal soap.

Commercial products can also be used to control soil diseases and pests. It is important to carefully read and follow the instructions to avoid damaging plants or contaminating the soil. Gardeners can also opt for homemade remedies, such as nettle brew or garlic infusions, to treat soil problems.

Another technique for managing soil diseases and pests is using companion plants. Certain plants can repel harmful insects or even attract their natural predators. For example, marigolds can repel aphids and attract ladybugs, which feed on them. Calendula and marigolds can also repel nematodes and whiteflies.

Finally, crop rotation can also help reduce soil diseases and pest problems. By regularly changing the location of plants, pests and diseases cannot establish and spread. Crop rotation also helps maintain a healthy and balanced soil by preventing nutrient depletion.

The Importance of Biodiversity and Garden Allies

Biodiversity is one of the most important elements of a healthy and fertile garden. It encompasses the complex interactions between plants, animals, microorganisms, and their environment, and plays a key role in maintaining plant health and soil fertility.

In a healthy ecosystem, each organism plays an important role in the life cycle and contributes to the regulation of pests and diseases. Garden allies, such as predatory insects, birds, and mammals, are integral parts of this ecosystem. Predatory insects like ladybugs and hoverflies feed on harmful insects that can damage crops and plants. Birds feed on insects and other small animals while dispersing seeds and pollinating plants. Mammals such as hedgehogs and shrews also help maintain a healthy soil by feeding on earthworms and other small animals.

It is essential to encourage biodiversity in your garden to promote the presence of these natural allies and reduce dependence on pesticides and other chemical products. Hedges, shrubs, and wildflowers provide habitats for allies, while aromatic plants like mint and lavender can repel certain harmful insects. Herbs and wildflowers also attract butterflies and bees, which play an important role in crop pollination.

It is also important to consider soil biodiversity. Microorganisms and earthworms are key players in soil health, and their presence can be encouraged through practices such as composting and cover cropping. Earthworms aerate the soil, improve drainage, and promote soil structure formation, while microorganisms decompose organic matter and release nutrients into the soil.

Identifying and Correcting Nutrient Deficiencies

To have a productive and healthy garden, it is essential to understand the nutrient deficiencies in your soil. Plants require a variety of nutrients to grow and develop, and if your soil is deficient in any of these elements, it can affect the health and yield of your plants. In this section, we will explore how to identify nutrient deficiencies and effectively and naturally correct them.

The first step in identifying nutrient deficiencies is to understand the signs that your plants may exhibit. Nutrient deficiencies often manifest as visual signs such as yellowing leaves, discolored or spotted leaves, stunted growth, or delayed flowering. Deficiencies can also be identified through soil analysis.

Soil analysis is a useful tool for understanding the nutrients available in your soil and potential deficiencies. Soil tests can be conducted using soil analysis kits or by sending a soil sample to an accredited laboratory. The results of soil analysis provide information on soil pH, nutrient levels such as nitrogen, phosphorus, and potassium, as well as organic matter levels.

Once nutrient deficiencies are identified, there are several ways to naturally correct them. The use of organic amendments such as compost, leaf litter, or green manures can improve the quality of your soil by providing essential nutrients and increasing organic matter content. The use of mineral amendments such as magnesium sulfate or limestone can also help correct nutrient deficiencies.

When applying amendments, it is important to consider soil pH. Soil pH plays a crucial role in nutrient availability to plants. If the soil is too acidic or alkaline, certain nutrients may be blocked, even if they are present in the soil. Therefore, it is important to correct soil pH before adding amendments.

Another way to correct nutrient deficiencies is by planning an effective crop rotation. Different plants have different nutritional needs, so by alternating crops, you can improve soil health and provide the nutrients that plants need to grow.

Finally, gardeners can also use specific fertilizers to correct nutrient deficiencies. Organic fertilizers like bone meal or guano can be used to provide specific nutrients, while mineral fertilizers can be used to supply essential nutrients such as nitrogen, phosphorus, and potassium.

Common Soil Problems and How to Solve Them

Acidic and Alkaline Soils: Causes and Consequences

Acidic and alkaline soils can be a real hindrance to plant growth and soil fertility. Acidic soils have a pH below 7, while alkaline soils have a pH above 7. Neutral soils have a pH of 7, which is considered ideal for most plants.

There can be multiple causes for acidic and alkaline soils. Acidic soils can be caused by high rainfall, excessive use of nitrogen fertilizers, natural soil acidification over time, or the presence of acidic rocks. Alkaline soils, on the other hand, can be caused by low rainfall, excessive irrigation, the presence of limestone in the soil, or excessive use of phosphate fertilizers.

The consequences of acidic and alkaline soils are numerous. Acidic soils can make essential nutrients for plants, such as nitrogen, phosphorus, and potassium, less available, which can result in insufficient plant growth. Acidic soils can also increase the toxicity of heavy metals present in the soil. Alkaline soils, on the other hand, can limit the availability of certain essential micronutrients, such as iron and manganese, which can also lead to insufficient plant growth.

Fortunately, it is possible to correct the pH of the soil by adding appropriate amendments. Acidic soils can be amended by adding lime or dolomite, while alkaline soils can be amended by adding sulfur or sulfuric acid. However, it is important to note that the process of correcting soil pH can be lengthy and may take several months.

It is also important to note that some plants are better suited to acidic or alkaline soils. For example, acid-loving plants such as blueberries and rhododendrons thrive in acidic soils, while alkaline-loving plants such as asparagus and carrots prefer alkaline soils. By choosing plants that are adapted to your soil, you can maximize the productivity of your garden.

Managing Salinity and Acidic or Alkaline Soils

Managing soil salinity and acidic or alkaline soils can be a real challenge for gardeners, but with the right techniques, it is possible to address these problems and produce healthy, vigorous plants.

Soil salinity can be caused by excessive irrigation or soils rich in minerals such as salt. To manage this problem, it is important to reduce the amount of water you provide to your plants and closely monitor the salt level in the soil. Adding organic matter can also help reduce salinity by improving soil structure and promoting the growth of beneficial microorganisms.

Acidic or alkaline soils can also affect plant growth. Acidic soils are often caused by excessive decomposing organic matter, while alkaline soils can be caused by soil rich in limestone or sodium bicarbonate. To address this problem, it is important to test the soil pH and adjust the amount of organic matter accordingly. In acidic soils, adding lime can help increase the pH, while in alkaline soils, adding sulfur can help reduce the pH.

It is also important to choose plants that are adapted to the conditions of your soil and climate. Some plants are more tolerant of saline, acidic, or alkaline soils than others. Succulent plants, for example, are well-suited to saline soils, while acid-loving plants include rhododendrons and blueberries. Alkaline-loving plants include asparagus and cabbage.

Compacted Soils: Causes, Consequences, and Solutions

Compacted soils can be a real challenge for gardeners. Compacted soil is soil where the pore space is reduced, limiting water and air infiltration, and thus restricting plant root growth. Compacted soils can be caused by various factors, including heavy vehicle traffic, repeated walking on the soil, animal trampling, and even rainfall. The consequences of compaction can be disastrous for plants, reducing their growth, vigor, yield, and disease resistance.

There are several solutions to address compacted soils. Prevention is always the best solution. Avoid walking on your soil when it is wet or moist, as this promotes compaction. Also, avoid heavy vehicle traffic on the soil. If you must use a lawnmower or tractors in your garden, try to use wider tires to reduce ground pressure.

If you already have compacted soil, there are several techniques to improve its structure. One is to regularly till your soil, especially at the beginning of the growing season. This will break up the compacted layer and improve soil porosity. You can also use a soil aerator, which creates holes in the soil to allow better water and air infiltration. Aeration is particularly useful for heavy and clay soils.

Another solution to improve soil structure is to use green manures or cover crops. The roots of these plants can help break up the compacted layer while adding organic matter to the soil. Cover crops can also help protect the soil from erosion and trap nutrients.

Finally, you can use soil amendments to improve the structure and fertility of your soil. Soil amendments can include organic materials such as compost, manure, or dead leaves, as well as mineral amendments such as limestone or gypsum. Adding these amendments can help improve soil porosity and provide nutrients to plants.

Polluted Soils: Causes, Consequences, and Solutions

Soil pollution is a major problem worldwide and has detrimental effects on the environment, human health, and agricultural productivity. Soils can be polluted by natural contaminants such as heavy metals or by human activities such as intensive agriculture, industry, and waste.

Polluted soils have negative effects on human health,

particularly on children who are more vulnerable to pollutants. Contaminants can enter the food chain by being absorbed by plants and animals, which can lead to serious health problems for those who consume them. Polluted soils can also have negative effects on biodiversity, reducing the diversity of species that inhabit the soil.

The solutions to address soil pollution vary depending on the nature and severity of the pollution. Remediation methods include chemical washing, thermal treatment, solvent extraction, and stabilization of contaminants in the soil. However, these methods are often expensive and can be challenging to implement on a large scale.

Another approach to address soil pollution is to use phytoremediation methods. This involves using specially selected plants to absorb contaminants from the soil, such as corn, sunflowers, and poplars. These plants have the ability to break down and eliminate pollutants, thereby restoring soil quality. Phytoremediation is a more cost-effective and sustainable method than traditional remediation methods.

Growing Plants Adapted to Your Soil and Climate

Choosing Resilient and Locally Adapted Varieties

Selecting plant varieties that are resilient and adapted to local conditions is crucial for maximizing soil fertility and increasing productivity in your garden. Plants that are well-adapted to the local environment have deeper roots, require less water, have better resistance to diseases and pests, and grow faster and healthier. As a result, they require less maintenance and produce abundant harvests.

To choose varieties that are suitable for your garden, it is important to consider different factors such as climate, soil, light, and exposure to wind. It is also important to consider your preferences in terms of cultivation and your production goals. To facilitate this step, you can consult seed and plant catalogs that are adapted to your region, as well as online information or experienced local gardeners.

By choosing varieties adapted to your soil and climate, you can reduce the risks of plant stress and diseases, as well as the need for irrigation and fertilization. For example, tomato plants adapted to hot and dry climates require less water and are more heat-resistant than varieties adapted to humid and cool climates. Insect-resistant cabbage varieties can reduce the need for chemical pesticide spraying. Native flower varieties attract local pollinators, which strengthen your garden's ecosystem and improve vegetable productivity.

Finally, it is important to consider the sustainability and diversity of your garden by choosing local and heirloom plant varieties. These varieties are often adapted to local conditions and have developed natural resistance to diseases and pests. Additionally, preserving these varieties can contribute to preserving the genetic diversity of plants and protecting food sovereignty.

The Importance of Pollination and Selecting Bee-Friendly Plants

Pollination is a vital process for the reproduction of plants and the production of fruits and vegetables. Without pollination, plants cannot produce seeds, which would make food production impossible. Insects, birds, bats, and even wind play a crucial role in pollinating plants. In a garden, it is important to promote pollination by choosing appropriate plants.

Bee-friendly plants are plants that produce nectar and pollen, making them attractive to bees and other pollinating insects. Bees are particularly important as they are responsible for pollinating most fruits and vegetables. By choosing bee-friendly plants for your garden, you can help attract bees and promote pollination.

Bee-friendly plants can be chosen based on the flowering period, color, and type of flowers. Plants that bloom early in spring are important for bees coming out of hibernation.

Plants with yellow, blue, and violet flowers are particularly attractive to bees. Single-flower plants, such as daisies, are easier for bees to pollinate compared to double-flower plants.

In addition to aiding pollination, bee-friendly plants can also have other benefits for your garden. Some bee-friendly plants, like lavender, can help repel harmful insects. Other plants, such as chamomile, have medicinal properties and can be used for herbal teas.

It is important to note that pesticides can harm bees and other pollinators. It is therefore preferable to use biological pest control methods in your garden. If you must use pesticides, make sure to do so responsibly and follow the instructions on the label.

Permaculture and the Design of Productive and Sustainable Gardens

Permaculture is a holistic approach to designing productive agricultural and garden systems that seek to mimic the patterns and processes of nature. It is based on ethical design principles that aim to create resilient and productive ecosystems in the long term while minimizing negative impacts on the environment.

Permaculture relies on diverse and integrated cultivation methods that aim to create a self-sustaining and sustainable system. The design of permaculture gardens integrates the use of biodiversity, crop rotation, companion planting, agroforestry, composting, water conservation, and other sustainable techniques to maximize garden productivity while preserving soil and environmental health.

Permaculture is an ecological and sustainable alternative to intensive farming methods that deplete the soil and natural resources. By incorporating ecological practices in garden design, permaculturists can reduce their ecological footprint while increasing food production.

One of the fundamental principles of permaculture is to work with nature rather than against it. Permaculturists seek to observe and understand the natural processes of the local ecosystem to design agricultural systems that adapt to the environment rather than seeking to dominate it. For example, instead of manually weeding or using herbicides, permaculturists use companion plants to suppress weeds and maintain fertile soil.

Permaculture gardens are designed to be resilient in the face of climate change and environmental challenges. By using water conservation techniques such as efficient irrigation systems and rainwater harvesting, permaculturists can maximize water usage while minimizing waste. Companion planting and crop rotation can also reduce the prevalence of diseases and pests while improving soil quality and productivity.

Finally, permaculture encourages the creation of local communities for sharing knowledge and experiences. Permaculture gardens are often designed to be communal spaces where people can meet, learn from each other, and share resources. This community-based approach also promotes mutual assistance and solidarity among community members.

Case Studies and Testimonials from Expert Gardeners

Successful experiences of gardens that have improved soil fertility

When it comes to soil fertility, it is important to understand that each garden is unique and requires specific care to achieve optimal results. However, it is also important to remember that certain basic principles can be applied to any garden to improve soil quality and maximize crop productivity. In this section, we will look at successful experiences from gardeners who have significantly improved the fertility of their soil.

The first key principle for improving soil fertility is to add organic matter. Gardeners who have succeeded in improving the fertility of their soil have used a variety of methods to add organic matter. Some have used homemade or store-bought compost, while others have used green manure or cover crops to add organic matter to their soil. Whatever method was used, the addition of organic matter helped increase the nutrient content of the soil and improve its structure, allowing plants to better root and absorb water and nutrients.

Another key principle for improving soil fertility is to use natural fertilizers. Gardeners who have succeeded in improving the fertility of their soil have used a variety of natural fertilizers, such as manure, guano, crushed eggshells, and seaweed. Natural fertilizers are rich in nutrients and help nourish the soil naturally, which can help stimulate plant growth and improve crop quality.

Another important strategy for improving soil fertility is to practice regular crop rotation. Gardeners who have succeeded in improving the fertility of their soil have found that crop rotation helps prevent soil nutrient depletion and promotes the growth of healthy and productive plants. By planting a variety of different crops each year, gardeners can help reduce the occurrence of diseases and pests and stimulate plant growth.

Lastly, gardeners who have succeeded in improving soil fertility have often implemented sustainable practices to manage water and soil resources. This can include techniques such as collecting rainwater, using mulch to retain moisture, and applying a layer of compost to help retain water in the soil. By using sustainable practices to manage soil resources, gardeners can help maintain soil quality in the long term and maximize the productivity of their garden.

Research projects and innovations in soil fertility

In the field of soil fertility, many research projects and innovations have been developed to improve the productivity of gardens and crops. These research and innovation projects have led to the discovery of new agricultural practices, tools, and techniques that have contributed to a better understanding of soil biology and how to harness it to maximize agricultural production. In this section, we will examine some of the most recent research and innovations in the field of soil fertility.

First, scientists have identified the importance of arbuscular mycorrhizal fungi for plant growth. These fungi live in symbiosis with plant roots and provide them with essential nutrients in exchange for sugars produced by the plants. Research has shown that plants that benefit from the association with these fungi are more resistant to diseases and have faster growth.

Next, there are biofertilizers, which are mixtures of beneficial microorganisms that contribute to soil fertility and improve plant growth. Biofertilizers contain nitrogen-fixing bacteria, phosphate-solubilizing bacteria, and mycorrhizal fungi. These beneficial microorganisms have a stimulating effect on plant growth and can enhance crop quality.

There are also natural products such as extracts of marine algae, which have stimulating properties for plant growth. Marine algae contain phytohormones and nutrients that promote seed germination, root growth, and photosynthesis.

Research has also shown that genetically modified plants can have a positive effect on soil fertility. For example, plants genetically modified to produce enzymes that break down organic matter in the soil can increase the organic matter content of the soil, improving its fertility and structure.

Finally, precision agriculture is another innovation that has an impact on soil fertility. Precision agriculture uses advanced technologies to monitor soil and plant conditions in real time, allowing for more efficient use of fertilizers and pesticides, reducing losses, and improving crop quality.

Experiences of farmers and professional gardeners

In this section, we will examine the experiences of farmers and professional gardeners in soil fertility. These testimonials are valuable because they can provide us with firsthand information about what works and what doesn't in practice. The experiences we will discuss here come from different regions, crops, and climatic conditions, but they all share an ecological and environmentally friendly approach.

A farmer I met in northern France uses an interesting technique to increase soil fertility. He plants legumes such as peas, beans, and alfalfa as cover crops between seasons. Legumes have the ability to fix nitrogen from the air and convert it into a usable nutrient for plants. This technique has not only increased the fertility of his soil but has also reduced his need for chemical fertilizers and external inputs.

Another farmer I met in South Africa uses a similar method by planting clover between crops. Clover is a cover crop that can also fix nitrogen from the air and enrich the soil with nutrients. In addition to increasing soil fertility, this method can also improve soil structure, reduce erosion, and promote biodiversity.

An urban gardener I met in Paris uses a composting method to improve soil fertility. He collects kitchen and garden waste, such as dead leaves, vegetable peelings, and grass clippings, and transforms them into compost. The compost is then used to enrich the soil with organic matter and nutrients, which stimulates plant growth and vegetable production.

Another gardener I met in London uses a technique called lasagna gardening. This technique involves layering organic materials, such as dead leaves, straw, and garden waste, to create a nutrient-rich soil. This method is simple, inexpensive, and can be used in small urban gardens to improve soil fertility.

These experiences show that increasing soil fertility can be achieved in different ways depending on the region, climate, and available resources. However, all these methods share an ecological and sustainable approach to plant cultivation, aiming to improve soil health, reduce costs, and increase vegetable and fruit production.

Tips and tricks from experienced gardeners

As an experienced gardener, I have learned many tips and tricks over the years to maximize soil fertility and the productivity of my garden. Here are some of my best tips for amateur gardeners:

Use kitchen waste as compost: Composting is an easy and inexpensive way to feed your soil with essential nutrients. You can add fruit and vegetable scraps, eggshells, and coffee grounds to your compost to help create nutrient-rich soil.

Plant cover crops: Cover crops are plants that are grown to cover the soil and improve its quality. They help protect the soil from erosion, increase organic matter content, and provide essential nutrients to other plants. Popular cover crops include clover, rye, and millet.

Use natural fertilizers: Natural fertilizers such as manure, compost, and seaweed are rich in essential nutrients and help improve soil quality. They are also more environmentally friendly than synthetic fertilizers.

Practice crop rotation: Crop rotation is an agricultural practice that involves changing the type of crop planted in a given area each year. This helps prevent soil nutrient loss and reduces exposure to diseases and pests.

Add organic matter: Organic matter is essential for soil health. It helps retain moisture, improve soil structure, and promote the growth of beneficial microorganisms. You can add organic matter to your soil by using natural fertilizers, cover crops, or plant residues.

Avoid overuse: Overusing your soil can deplete its essential nutrients and reduce its quality. Try not to plant the same crops in the same place every year and avoid trampling or compacting your soil.

Test your soil: Soil analysis can help you understand the nutrient needs of your soil and determine appropriate amendments to make. Soil test kits are available in garden stores, or you can contact a specialized soil analysis laboratory.

Pay attention to your plants' water needs: Water is essential for plant growth, but too much or too little water can cause problems. Try not to overwater and make sure not to let your soil become too dry or too wet.

Use mulching techniques: Mulching is a technique that involves covering the soil with organic materials such as straw, leaves, or bark. This helps preserve soil moisture, reduce weed growth, and improve soil quality by adding organic matter.

Avoid pesticides and chemicals: Pesticides and chemicals can be harmful to beneficial microorganisms in the soil. Try to avoid them as much as possible and use natural methods of pest and disease control, such as companion planting and natural predators.

Be patient: Building fertile soil takes time and requires consistent effort. Be patient and persistent in your gardening practice to achieve lasting results.

Lastly, remember that every garden is unique and requires a personalized approach. Feel free to experiment and adjust your gardening practices based on the specific needs of your soil and plants. Good luck in your gardening practice!

Acknowledgment

With deep emotion and a certain nostalgia, I stand before you, dear reader, at the end of this exciting journey we have embarked on together. This book, «Mastering the Secrets of Fertile Soil to Maximize Your Garden's Productivity,» is the result of many years of research, reflection, and hard work. First and foremost, I want to express my gratitude to each and every one of you for reading these pages to the very end and for sharing this adventure with me.

Like rain nourishes the soil and brings forth seeds, your encouragement and curiosity have nourished my passion for soil fertility and garden biology. Drawing from the experience of countless gardeners and experts, exploring the intricacies of science, and learning from ancient traditions, I have crafted this book. My aim was to offer you innovative and thought-provoking insights, practical tips, and inspiring anecdotes to guide you in the art and science of cultivating fertile and productive soil.

I would like to thank all the individuals who have contributed to enriching this book with their knowledge, advice, and testimonials. Their generosity and passion for gardening have been an invaluable source of inspiration and motivation. The roots of this book run deep in the fertile soil of their experiences and teachings.

To you, dear reader, I extend my heartfelt thanks for taking the time to immerse yourself in these pages. I hope this book has brought you new knowledge, inspiring ideas, and effective techniques to improve your soil's fertility and your garden's productivity. Just as an attentive gardener shapes the earth, I hope to have sown in you the seeds of a renewed passion for gardening and for the preservation of our precious natural resources.

Lastly, I invite you to continue exploring, experimenting, and sharing your discoveries and successes in the art of cultivating fertile and productive soil. Remember that gardening is a path filled with learning, surprises, and joys. Together, let us cultivate our passion for the earth and plants, and may our gardens bloom with a thousand colors and flavors.

Once again, thank you from the bottom of my heart for your trust and support. May you find in this book the inspiration and knowledge to turn your garden into a true paradise, where life blooms abundantly and fertile soil generously offers its benefits.